8-19-06

Blessings to Freddie, a very talented & beautiful Lady. Peace, Love & Light

Little Anthony

FROM THE GROUND UP

BY
Per'le Oliver

Bloomington, IN   Milton Keynes, UK

AuthorHouse™
1663 Liberty Drive, Suite 200
Bloomington, IN 47403
www.authorhouse.com
Phone: 1-800-839-8640

AuthorHouse™ UK Ltd.
500 Avebury Boulevard
Central Milton Keynes, MK9 2BE
www.authorhouse.co.uk
Phone: 08001974150

© 2006 Per'le Oliver. All rights reserved.

No part of this book may be reproduced, stored in a retrieval system, or transmitted by any means without the written permission of the author.

First published by AuthorHouse 5/18/2006

ISBN: 1-4259-3404-8 (sc)

Library of Congress Control Number: 2006904151

Printed in the United States of America
Bloomington, Indiana

This book is printed on acid-free paper.

ACKNOWLEDGEMENTS

Special thanks to: Brian Mattox of Author House, for your expertise, patience and for such a joyous experience and making this publication possible.

I would like to thank my husband who has traveled every mile with me through all of my endeavors with love, support and patience's. My mother, Irene Dismuke for her, love, encouragement, inspiration, and belief in me. My Father Major Bluford, thanks to you that I am the individual, wife, mother and free spirit of today . My daughter Veronica Lynn Hatton for her expertise, love, loyalty, spiritual insight and is truly a blessing to me. My daughter Cynthia Oliver for her love, support, caring and sharing attitude. My Son Roger II and daughter in- law Renee, always supportive, faithful, and encouraging in all that I do. My son Allan Silas who made this venture possible due to his financial support, love and patience, Son, Allan II and daughter in - law Patricia for their loyalty, love and support, Grand daughters, Kelly Renee Craig (a published author) and very supportive and knowledgeable. Forsnica Lynn Hatton, for her loyalty, support, love, taking the time to critique my work, and sticking with me in all that I do, Marcie and Krystal for their support, love and faith in me. Grand Son, Lakey, Roger III, Brad and Allan III. All of my great-grand's, Daniel, Dalero, Diyale, Dava'Reyon, Destiny, Deshun, Diamond, and Safaria. My sister Linda Dozier, for her love, support, laughter, and encouragement, my brother-in-law Art Dozier(a very talented writer) thanks for sharing the knowledge and giving encouragement. My brother, Tony Dismuke & wife Linda for their love and support, Aunt Annie B. Sykes, for so much love and appreciation. Doris Ballinger (friend of forty-seven years}, Emma Johnson and Willa Oliver, MacArthur and Mary Helen Billings, Corine Ratliff (friend since childhood), Geraldine Baker, Cecil and Pecola Robinson, Geraldine Wilder, Angela Dismuke, Pattie Longo, Robert and Jean White, Mose and Carol White, Charles Adams, and Andrew Jackson, and my guardian angel, Dawn Jackson and daughters, Larry and Roxanne Green, Ray and Fay Robinson. Emma Jean Hoskins, Matilda Harrington, Dr. Ernestine Harrington, Roy Lee, Billie, Melvin Walters and Nathaniel.

The Clan of:

Tom & Catherine Howard, Fr. William Oliver, The Billings, The Tatums, Ben Mitchell, Pearl White, The Blufords, Percy and Frank Sykes, Corine Taylor, Corine Adams, Sula Ford, Viola Hart, The Ratliffs, and Rich Washington.

Dr. V. Borromeo, Thank you for your dedication, loyalty and unspoken spirituality, Mary and Alicia for your loving and kind spirit. Dr. Arnold Gross, Dr Jyothi Kadambi and Dr. Chas. Innis and

Sharon, Thank you for your dedication to your profession.

Spiritual Institutes
The Spiritual Israel Temple #2 Church. Bishop Tillman Oliver, Elder William Oliver, Mo. Claudia, Elder Michael Oliver, Mo. Tina, Rev. Mark Oliver, Rev. Geraldine Cochran and Rev James Lathan of Detroit, Michigan, Mo. Ophelia Johnson, Bertha Crosby, Leroy Oliver, and Mo Vera Martin and all of the congregation.

The Alhambra Institute, Alexia and Stephen of Dearborn, Michigan and Coldwater, MI. Thank you for all of the spiritual teachings, sharing a lifetime of knowledge. It is because of your teachings that I know my path in life. May you have twenty plus more years as owners of The Alhambra Institute. Your teachings were the beginning of my spirituality.

International Center for Reiki, Master William L. Rand, of Southfield, Michigan and an extraordinary instructor and spiritually endowed.

Ferndale Community Center, Barbara Miller of Ferndale, Michigan. Thank you for your confidence, support and loyalty.

Positive Living Consultant Group of Southfield, MI

Yvonne Hodge, James Hodge, Allan Oliver, Lynell Crew, Gail Embery, Sharon Marshall D. Min., and Cathy Parnell. Thank you for your loyalty and spiritual teachings.

Circles of Lights, A course in Miracles Group of Southfield, MI

Special thanks to my friend of forty- seven years Flora N. Wilson, Carolyne "Isis" Fuqua (a published author) Ph. D., And Lucille Lloyd. Thank you for sharing your excellence as spiritual mentors.

Mystical Gardens, Margaret Smith, of Highland Park, MI. Thank you for your friendship, knowledge, and intuitive ability as Spiritual advisor.

New Life Vision Ministry/Christian Women of Glow Ministries. Dr. Ernestine Harrington, of Detroit, MI. Thank You for your friendship, dedication, and Spiritual incite.

Communication Specialist Computers, Andrew Wallace and Shane Irving. Thank you for your professionalism and kindness.

The Eldorado Searchers Club throughout the U.S. Thank you for an excellent job of keeping us together.

In Memory of: Mo. Barbie L. Howard Billings, Acie Billings, Major and Mitty Bluford, Fr. William and Mo.Willie B. Oliver, Lacy and Thomas Billings, Major Bluford III, Roger Ballinger Sr., Ernest Dismuke, Br. Mo Hattie Oliver, and Lonie Johnson, Wm Oliver, Jim Longo, Percel Loggin, Nathaniel Howard, Melvatine Cephas, Willie Bluford, Birdie Bluford, Yvette Cox, Percy, Frank and Annie Sykes, Lucille, Ben, and Ambrose Mitchell.

CONTENTS

MY CONTRACT 1

OTHER SIDE OF RAINBOWS 2

ANGEL 3

DELETING "MR D" 4

THE WONDERS OF WATERMARKS 5

BELIEVE 6

AS I LIVE EACH DAY 7

THE SONG I NEVER WROTE
FOR MY FATHER 8

SEA STORMS 9

A FRIEND FOR FLORA 10

KINGFISH THE FIGHTING ROOSTER 11

HIS QUEEN 12

KARMA 13

MYSTICAL LADY 14

MY ORCHID 15

BIG I'S AND LIL U'S 16

GRAMA PLEASE ! NOT MY PET PIG 17

DO YOU KNOW ME ? 18

WISHFUL THINKING 19

LIL BRO 20

DAY AFTER TOMORROW	21
WOMAN SCORNED ??	22
THE FAITH OF FEW	23
THE FOLLOWER	24
CAN I SHARE MY THOUGHTS	25
BEAUTY THE CHICKEN THIEF	26
YOU ARE JEALOUSY	27
A BABYSITTING NIGHTMARE	28
SELF LOVE	29
AFFIRMATION FOR SELF	30
HUSBAND	33
ROGER II	34
VERONICA	35
ALLAN S.	36
ALLAN	37
CYNTHIA	38
LINDA (BAY)	39
MOM	40
IRENE	41
ARTHUR	42
TONY	43
RENEE	44
PATRICIA	45

LINDA	46
DANIEL	47
KELLY	48
FORSNICA	49
MARCIE	50
KRYSTAL	51
LAKEY	52
ROGER III	53
FANNIE	54
JUSTIN	55
ANGELO	56
RONNIE	57

MY CONTRACT

I'm standing on the corner you could have been me
I signed a contract between me and thee
I ask for spare change everyday
Cause I am a lost soul who can't find its way
I live under bridges come rain or snow
Very few of you sisters and brothers really know
My karma is to live this life
I know I won't ever thrive
But when I'm through
I may pass it on to you.

OTHER SIDE OF RAINBOWS

Other side of rainbows that's where I'll make my home
Where grass is so green and flowers are so true
And all of nature whispers I love you
On the other side of rainbows
Trees grow tall and mountains don't fall
Fireflies don't light
And little boys fly their kites
Where Angels dwell and the devil from hell, patiently awaits his sinners
But not one soul, not even the beginners
Ever planned to enter
No crying skies, no burning sun
Singing joyful songs from dusk till dawn

ANGEL

The Angel of life calls my name
Out of the light she swiftly came
She knew not I to blame
When I cried," help me now to understand fame"
Closer and closer to me she came, whispering in my ear
Fame, fortune, and earthly possessions
Can only build ugly obsessions
It was never yours to keep
So when you leave it please do not weep.
Her words penetrated slow
But finally I decided to let go
I knew I had to make that choice
I had heard the angel's voice
I had been safe up until then
Because I knew she wouldn't be back again.

DELETING "MR D"

Divorcing yourself from negativity

Expressing self Love

Picturing the positive

Realization of self image

Expect a miracle

Sustain your efforts

See the beauty in life

Imagine a picture perfect life

One with God

Never conform to your symptoms of depression

THE WONDERS OF WATERMARKS

I am the watermarks on your paper, forming
pictures, images of people, Animals, and numbers,
Telling someone's future that has yet to unfold
The secrets I can no longer withhold
Free spirit, free energy
Challenging the world of its decisions and choices
Images, people, animals, numbers brought to life
Without difficulty or strife
Feeling free and striking, when forming life with
type
Waiting patiently to be chosen
Without a single word spoken
In error ball me up and throw me away
My friends will join you another day
Since nothing can last forever, this is good bye but
I won't cry.

BELIEVE

Believing that you can, but never do
Fearing that it's not for you
Saying that you will never be
Ignoring the promises that could be
Arise each morning give thanks
For all of your gifts stored in your spiritual bank
Withdrawals are easily made
For those of us who are not easily swayed
So when you decide that you can do
And began to think that it's just for you
Say it will always be
Realize he cannot tell a lie
And would never pass you by
Give thanks, believing all of your needs are met
Not for one moment will you fret

AS I LIVE EACH DAY

As I live each day, I will give thanks for all of my blessings
As I live each day I will glorify God's holy name
As I live each day I will love those who have wronged me
As I live each day I will love unconditionally
As I live each day I will not be superficial
As I live each day I will forgive those who are judgmental toward me
As I live each day I will try to be a blessing to someone
As I live each day I will de-press all negative vibrations
As I live each day I will de- nounce fear and dis-ease from my life
As I live each day I will bestow blessings and healings upon myself and others as requested
As I live each day I will choose the choices that God has made for me and live by them
As I live each day I will be a conquer and never a failure
As I live each day I will learn from those that I can learn from and teach those that I can
As I live each day I will love myself
As I live each day I will forgive myself.

THE SONG I NEVER WROTE FOR MY FATHER

You went away when I was two,
I've missed you so, I still love you,
You never tried
To stand by my side
I want you to know how much I cried
You've taken the part
That once was my heart
Now you are an old man about to depart
You never knew from day to day
If mom would even get a pay
So you went on to build, a brand new life
Taking on a new wife
Many children you had
Always Standing by their side
If it hadn't been for God I surely would have died
But I have been more blessed than all of your rest
So, with this, my best
I just wanted to write this song that I never wrote to
You---my father.

SEA STORMS

Sea storms, sea storms clouding my eyes into consciousness
I fear not the storm will come again today
Maybe tomorrow
The heavens opens up to ingest all of the sorrows of the earth
So bright, until nightfall again
Mangled spirits invades us and now we are engulfed with the storms of today.

A FRIEND FOR FLORA

Sunday mornings as we sat at the kitchen table
Expressing our fears and doubts
Expelling bitterness, embracing joy
Crying through the bad times
Laughing and rejoicing through the good
Never thinking of growing old
And not knowing that aging would prove more valuable than gold
Wisdom and knowledge would take a seat
And this we would gracefully greet
So thankful that some lessons would not repeat
When we spoke of fears and doubts
Not realizing that it was God, who had all the clout
Down through the years
Through many tears
We learned to face our fears and conquer our doubts
So sad, so many dear to us had to leave
Without embracing a life of ease
We played the part of the wise
You could see the sincerity in our eyes
We thought it wise and would say
"Stop the world I want to get off today"
Foolish in so many ways
So happy to say, long gone those days

KINGFISH THE FIGHTING ROOSTER

Kingfish was a gorgeous multi colored Rooster
who lived in our next door neighbor's back yard,
she cock a doodle do all night
I do believe he did it for spite
I tossed him corn during the day
But I knew he wanted to eat all through the night
He would meet me at the gate waiting to fight
Anyone entered, from them he would take a bite
Scratches on my legs and all over my arms
I never dreamed he would do me harm
Ungrateful, that he was
I could clearly see, he didn't care a darn about me
Even little children he would fight
And then late one summer night, someone took Kingfish away
A big neighborhood feast we had the very next night
None spoke of Kingfish's fate
Because when he left it was in dark of night and very late.

HIS QUEEN

She was only sixteen, his teenage queen
Lost and turned out
He was her king, always in her dreams
No fear of God he said, tis only a name
To believe in that you gotta be insane
She never thought she would get old
Never thought he could turn so cold
His fate of death surrounded his bed
She could hear him talking out of his head
What's gonna happen to her, in her senior years
For when she was young, she did not fear
Now she is fifty, nowhere to run, nowhere to hide
She cried, Oh God is it too late to abide
What a fool she had been
Not even a next of kin
Abused, misused, life destroyed beyond repair
So sad how nobody cared,
She knew that she had to survive
In God she put her trust
Survive she did, no options left except to simply abide.

KARMA

So you think that I need to learn a Karmic lesson
Oh, that's ok with me because I know those
lessons are blessings
I will not do to you, as you have done to me
I know that is not life's key
I will surround myself with pure love
So that I can receive my blessings from above
When I submit my requests into the universe
Blessings it shall return, not a curse
Gift and fruit of the spirit is what I need
I don't have to get down on my knees and plead
Karmic lessons I have a few and I'm willing to pay
I just pray its not today.

MYSTICAL LADY

Mystical lady do it right
Not all can read with sheer delight
The clock on the wall says twelve midnight
I can see you're good at what you do
That is why so many come to you
Tell me about the spirit that's sitting on my knee
And tell her I don't want to see
If you can make her go away
I will give you a full days pay
And then the one to my right
Tell him he's gripping me too tight
And when they leave, don't come back
Cause I'm sick and tired of all that ghostly yak yak
yak

MY ORCHID

My heart smiles when I see the leaves dancing to the melody of the warm summer breeze
As I walked through my private orchid I could smell the freshness of the fruit trees
The trail leading through the orchid was covered with clay dirt and earth's red sand
To keep my hair in tact I wore a red head band
As I passed on through, there was not one green plum already bloomed
But I did see a possum and a coon
So with my brown bag in one hand and the table salt in the other
I was ready to eat green plums from the tree and other fruit from the vine
As I examined all the vines
Now ready to dine
I was disappointed that all of trees and vines were bare
The ants, lizards and grasshoppers didn't seem to care.

Big I's and Lil U's

How would it be if birds couldn't sing?
No air to breathe
No flowers in spring
No rivers or streams
Mountains crumble your world tumble
Flames falling from the sky
No more tears to cry
Nobody to blame
No such thing as fame
Everybody suffers, your world comes to an end
Holding little faith, the best you can
Down from your cloud to the lowest level
Now you realize, you couldn't have stayed there forever
All of a sudden you believe in devil
No more big I's and LiL U's
This ain't no psych I use
I just got the news
It's time to pay dues
No more who's who
No more favors for just you
This notice I read
So you'd better take heed
No more of your evil deeds, cause
As of tonight god has gone on strike.

GRAMA PLEASE ! NOT MY PET PIG

That big fat wooden table leg in my Grama's
kitchen was my very special place
I listen intensely to Grama's friends that came to
visit every evening
They told of their work day, some even gossiped
Ghost stories rang over kitchen wall
Through the house, down the hall
I was so glad when they went home
I thought that I had heard it all, but must have
missed, the plans to eat my pet pig
Black night falling, as I sat stroking my kitty cat
With greasy and loose lips
They danced, pranced and dipped
Around in the yard some began to skip
Others played with cards
Grama played her part
and straight from her heart, as she turned toward
me with tears in her eyes
She called out "COME AND GIT IT"

DO YOU KNOW ME ?

I am the light of your life
I am the epitome of time
I am one with the creator
I am of the South, East, North and West
I am the universe
I am happiness
I am freedom and forgiveness
I am your heaven on earth
I am faithfulness and truth
I am generosity, patience, and peace
I am the greatest gift you could ever possess
I am unconditional love.

WISHFUL THINKING

My husband Oli and I get out of bed at 6:00am every morning, after Toast and Coffee, this is our daily routine:

7:00 - 9:00am Go to the mall and walk around for two hours.
10:00 - 11:00am go exercise class.
11:30am - 12: 45pm go to Dance Class.
1:00pm Lunch, a salad with low fat dressing and three 16oz. Glasses of water.
3:00pm Walk ten blocks to get our granddaughter Nic, from school this is twenty blocks round trip.
4:00 - 4:30pm sit down, prop feet up and relax.
5:00 - 6- 00pm Dinner, 1 slice wheat bread, 1 med. Baked Potato, 1cup vegetable or lettuce salad, 1 med. Baked Chicken Breast.
7:00pm Do the washing , Ironing, vacuum the house we share all of the house work.
9:00pm If summertime we cut, rake, bag up the cut grass and edge the lawn.
If winter we shovel the snow.
11:30pm we get out bath or shower, lay our clothes out for the next day and kiss each other good night.
Since we are senior citizens we know the chances are greater that we may die in our sleep, but we are working extra hard to die healthy.

LIL BRO

My little brother, if my heart could sing
It would sing a song as beautiful as the Rainforest in May
I'd make each day
A special day for me and for you, if my heart could sing.
In every flower
I can see your face
But now I know it's just empty space
My imaginary place
From your special world
I can hear your heart sing
And when you sing
The soft sound of chimes
Melody of old times
When your heart sing you haven't a care
But with me your spirit can still share
So when you hear my heart sing
So much joy it's bound to bring
To my heart in spring
I will know that special day
When I hear your heart sing

DAY AFTER TOMORROW

Grama picked the cotton
Found most of it rotten
Cause the big red snake had ate his fill
He couldn't break her will
but she did feel ill
She'd had her fill, of taking all them pills
As she went to the other side of the field
Old sun came out
But soon went back
As Grama slowly filled her sack
Rain drenched her well
You could hardly tell
She was getting sicker by the day
Too sick to say
I got to git my pay
Cause I got to pay my bills
To collect her pay, she had to crawl up a hill
She knew she'd never make it
Grama's sixth sense had served her well
She knew it was just a matter of time
Her clock was running down, she fell to the ground
Dimmer and dimmer
Not a speck of glimmer
Angels came to her side
She had no fear to hide
She grew so weak, she could hardly speak
And she knew it was day after tomorrow.

WOMAN SCORNED ??

Go forth and bring thee, the object of my affection
upon my turf
Be not ashame to conjure the hand full of stars
that meant us be
Once long ago we sacrificed as one
Dreams faded away like the ocean waves
Taking deep gulps, until everything unexisted
The deeds do I to you horrific
But think not of the past remnants
Let us just appreciate the love of vibes now here
Perhaps it was not meant to be, for in my house
there is a valley scorned as I so doeth
But still I will wait in awareness that your return
not.

THE FAITH OF FEW

Give me the faith to believe that
All of my needs and desires are met before they reach me
All of my concerns are already solved
Give me the assurance that all of my hopes and dreams are of your approval
Give me the mentality to believe that all things that comes to me are from the spirit world
And all of my needs have been met
As I speak they are materializing into my physical world
Help me to live each day to walk by faith, not by sight.

THE FOLLOWER

My friends all talk loud
I had to follow the crowd
I had this fear of being alone
So I went to school just to act a fool
Popularity was my goal
Not trying to be bold
But my grades went down
Family problems all around
Only God knew, where I was bound
I followed my friends and committed a sin
Got caught in the act and went straight to jail
The judge set my bail
I had to stay in jail
What a mess for a girl !
Nearly ruined my world
I still regret to this very day
Causing so much pain
So I went back to school
But not to act a fool
Got my degree and now I can see
What my mom was saying to me
So if you feel your friends love is real
Stand back, so you can see the real deal
One friend in a lifetime and you are tops
Cause too many friends and you're going to meet the cops.

CAN I SHARE MY THOUGHTS

Can I share my thoughts with you
Can I share my dreams with you
Lately you don't seem to care
About the dreams we use to share
Life is but a slow ticking clock
Surely running down, down, down
Thank God, I won't get old all alone
Met a friend the other day
Said he was still in love with me
Told me his problems, I told him mines too
And guess what, after that he didn't seem so blue
He offered me a date
I said no thanks
Told him that I could never go out on you
When the tables turn
I hope you'll say, "no thanks too"

BEAUTY THE CHICKEN THIEF

Beauty was a beautiful brown shaggy dog and my best friend, she would bark and scratch the door wanting to come inside. House rules were, no pets inside.
Beauty was very special, she had the intelligence of a human. Early every Sunday mornings Beauty would disappear. When she reappeared, she'd wag her tail and wait for me to give her a loving pat on the head.
After she got her pat on the head, she go around to the side of the house and to my surprise she'd grace the household with a big fat juicy chicken.
Into the frying pan it would go
Frying not too fast
But sort of slow
Beauty was happy, so I'd been told
But the truth was Beauty's story had not unfolded.
The next Sunday morning Beauty went out, but she had no chicken when she came back
Instead she had been badly burned
Poor Beauty passed on
Beauty had to pay the Karma for being a thief
When she comes back she probably won't repeat.

YOU ARE JEALOUSY

You are staring at me from head to toe
And you haven't even noticed your lips dragging the floor
Everybody can plainly see
That you just can't help being jealous of me
You talk about my makeup
You say I look false
But honey, you look like King Kong's boss
You crawl out of bed
Looking almost dead
Everybody round you, is just plain scared
Yo eyes so red
Yo teeth so bucked
You don't even know you just straight out of luck
Next time you see a high stepper like me
Keep a stiff upper lip
Ya might git a good tip.

A BABYSITTING NIGHTMARE

My babysitter's house sat upon the hill
I hated those days
It took much power of will
Two big snuff stained teeth
She just loved smiling at me
Spat in my eyes and I could hardly see
Slop jar on the side of her bed
I slipped on the mess and hit my head
Victrola in the corner and records on the floor
She played music, dance around me until I began to weep
There was one thing I did know, this babysitting job she couldn't keep
The clock struck five
I tried to dive out the door
I was trying hard to get my stride
Big thump, little thump
I hit the floor and didn't quite make it to the door
I was desperately trying to survive
Oh God, I had nowhere to hide
Her dog took pity
Her teeth were gritty
She drug me away
Sharp pain all over my skin
This had to be the end
With this I knew, I would never go there again.

SELF LOVE

People will say that you are foolish
Because you love your self
People will say that you are selfish
Because you love yourself
People will say that you are not capable of loving
your fellow man
Because you love yourself
People will say that you are only a legend in your
own mind
Because you love yourself
People say that you can never be
Because you love yourself
You ARE,
Because you love yourself
Thank you for this wonderful love
I do love myself.

AFFIRMATION FOR SELF

I BELIEVE that THROUGH GOD we can do all things.
I BELIEVE that WITHOUT God we can do no-things.
I BELIEVE that what our mind can conceive, we can achieve. (if we can think of it, we can do it, because everything starts with a thought).
I BELIEVE that everyone has a very special gift, and it is our free will and choice to develop it.
I BELIEVE that all of our needs, hopes, dreams and desires are (manifested) met in the spirit world and will materialize in the physical world (earth).
I BELIEVE that if we remain strong in our beliefs and do not doubt, our desires will materialize (come to us quicker).
I BELIEVE that we can face our fears and conquer our doubts.
I BELIEVE that when we ask God, the Universe for something, we must ask, step back and give him enough time to work it out and not try to make it happen our way, let him do it his way.
I BELIEVE THAT GOD'S time frame is different from ours, He works by his time not ours therefore, we should not expect to receive anything when we think that we are ready.
I BELIEVE that when God feels that we are ready for our prayers to be answered he will then permit it to happen.

I BELIEVE that we must walk by faith and not by sight, (BELIEVING with our mind and in our heart that we already have (whatever it is that we are praying for) although, WE DO NOT YET SEE IT, (this does not matter) because I BELIEVE with all of my heart and all of my soul that I WILL see it and have it.

I BELIEVE that we must stay clear and away from negative talking people, places, and things in order for our blessings to manifest in the spirit and materialize in our world.

I BELIEVE that association with negative people will block our blessings.

I BELIEVE that negative people possess great powers((energy), when they release their negative thoughts, words,and deeds out into the universe (if we are in their association), their aura will pull us into their negativity and it can destroy our faith, hopes, dreams, and blessings

I BELIEVE we must love everyone, look for love and goodness in them regardless as to what walk of life they are from (no exceptions), in order for God work his miracles in our life.

I BELIEVE that God created us all and he loves us all equally.

I BELIEVE that each of us will incur Karmic situations that has to be paid back to the universe. If we incur positive Karma. We will receive positive karma, if we incur negative Karma we will receive negative Karma in our lives.

I BELIEVE that Karma is whatever we give out, is what we will get back. (If we give negative

actions, we will get back negative reactions, If we give positive actions, we will get back positive reactions).
I DO NOT BELIEVE that Karma is punishment, I DO BELIEVE that Karma exist only to teach us the lessons that we need to learn.
Peace, Love, and Life

HUSBAND

Handsome
Unique
Spiritually evolved
Brilliant
Audacious
Nobility
Determination

ROGER II

Respectable / Responsive
Observant / Omnisciency
Gallant / Generous
Encouraging
Righteousness

VERONICA

Virtuous
Elegant
Radiant
Omnipotent
Needs TLC
Individuality
Creative
Attractive

ALLAN S.

Affectionate / Artistic
Loving / Luminous
Loyalty
Analytical
Nobility
Spirituality

ALLAN

Attentive
Logical
Loving
Admirable
Needs TLC

CYNTHIA

Creative
Youthful
Needs TLC
Tranquil
Harmonious
Intelligent
Angelic

LINDA (BAY)

Loving
Illuminating
Needs TLC
Devoted
Adorable

MOM

My loving Madere
Omnipotent
Metaphysically spiritual

IRENE

Inspiring
Realistic
Expressive
Needs TLC
Exhilarating

ARTHUR

Artistic
Resonance
Tactful
Humble
Undeniable
Resourceful

TONY

Trustworthy
Observant
Naturalistic
Young at heart

RENEE

Reputable
Enchanting
Needs TLC
Entertaining
Elite

PATRICIA

Patient
Attentive
Tactful
Respectful
Intelligent
Conservative
Intriguing
Artistic

LINDA

Loveable
Independent
Nutritive
Dependable
Astonishing

DANIEL

Distinctiveness
Artistic
Needs TLC
Intelligent
Extraordinary
Level headed

KELLY

Knowledgeable
Eloquent
Loyal
Loving
Young at heart

FORSNICA

Fabulous
Omnipotent
Resonant
Spiritual
Noble
Intelligent
Creative
Attractive

MARCIE

Magnanimous
Adorable
Ravishing
Colorful personality
Intelligence
Elegant

KRYSTAL

Kindness
Realistic
Youthful
Spiritual
Talented
Articulate
Loving

LAKEY

Lovable
Anointed
Kind
Eminent
Young man

ROGER III

Resourceful
Outgoing
Gracious
Engaging
Reflective

FANNIE

Friendly
Ambitious
Nimble
Nurturing
Intelligent
Enthusiastic

JUSTIN

Justifiable
Understanding
Sensible
Tactful
Independent
Needs TLC

ANGELO

Anointing
Nature loving
Generous
Expressive
Loving
Outgoing

RONNIE

Responsible
Obliging
Noble
Naturalistic
Intelligent
Eccentric

ABOUT THE AUTHOR

Perle was born in Eldorado, Arkansas and raised by her grandmother until age eleven. At this age, she moved to Detroit, Michigan to live with her mother, stepfather, and little sister. She lives with her husband, Allan and youngest son Allan Silas. Perle and her husband has nine children
Allan Jr., Roger Jr., Cynthia, Veronica, Allan Silas, Justin, Angelo, Ronnie and Lawrence.

Perle became a member of "The Alhambra Institute" in Dearborn, Michigan and studied Metaphysics for a number of years, and later started to teach and do spiritual readings there. This is where her spiritual education and training beginned. She had always been a skeptic about unseen forces, but in learning how to access the source of universal knowledge, she became a true believer. She is a firm believer that every human being is spiritually gifted and the only thing needed is to tap into the divine path through the affirmations in this book of poems.

Perle teaches Metaphysics and is a certified hypnotherapist with" The Alhambra Institute". She has received certification as a Reiki healer from The International Center for Reiki Training"; through this training she learned that the body is a healing agent and how to use its energies. Perle is also affiliated with Ferndale Community Center as an Instructor, The Positive Living consultants organization and Circles of Light (A course in Miracles), and The Spiritual Israel Church Temple #2. All of these organizations compliments the other, she believes "if you want Knowledge you have to find it, without spiritual knowledge you are but a spiritual midget".

She wrote this book in hopes of being instrumental in helping you to accomplish the necessities in life as well as your hopes and dreams. She hopes you will laugh a little and it is ok to cry a little.

The author can be contacted at:
fromthegroundup@perleoli.com

Printed in the United States
55411LVS00001B/30